A Refuge of Tales

Lynne Sargent

A REFUGE OF TALES ©2020 by Lynne Sargent. All rights reserved. No part of this book may be used or reproduced in any manner whatsoever without written permission except in the case of brief quotations in critical articles and reviews. For more information, contact Renaissance Press. First edition.

Cover art by Robyn Lightwalker, design by Nathan Fréchette.

Interior design by Nathan Fréchette.

Edited by L.P. Vallée, Jade Crevier and Joel Balkovec.

Legal deposit, Library and Archives Canada, October 2020.

Paperback ISBN 978-1-987963-97-7

Ebook ISBN 978-1-987963-98-4

Renaissance Press

http://pressesrenaissancepress.ca

pressesrenaissancepress@gmail.com

We acknowledge the support of the Canada Council for the Arts and the Ontario Arts Council.

A Refuge of Tales

Lynne Sargent

This book is for anyone who has ever needed a new story to get them through a long night.

Repeat

There are two ways of making myths;

for the first:
      kiss a sunset
      feel its colour
      on your lips, hold
      your lover's hand

      repeat.

the second:
      tell a lie to a child
      watch them build
      it into truth, tell it
      again

      believe.

Part 1: A Myth of Women

For women who want to know the shape of the monsters they sleep with

The candle is an itch,
a plucked loose thread,
a hangnail.

The tallow might burn,
might whisk all there is away
but at least her mind will be made smooth as well—
she will know.

There will be no more jagged edge
that might stab, no thread
that might unravel.

There will be no more nagging
questions that will not let
a nerve, a brain,
quiet.

You assume we should fear the punishment
for our transgressions, that we should not
choose the certain suffering,
but suffering is the only thing we have
no uncertainty about.

We only end the purgatory,
the fear, that the man might easily
be worse than the bear.

We rip that question away with gritted teeth,
unmask him so we may sleep once again
in the cold, unquestioned,
quiet.

 Kingly

There have been a thousand nights,
A thousand 'not tonight's.

A thousand mornings you have
not chopped off my head.
A thousand mornings I have
kept it.

I have told myself a thousand stories
so that I will not have to fear
the tomorrows

will not have to wonder when it will come.

There have been a thousand mornings
where you have seen only your own
hurt

instead of your womanless country,
the suffering, the daughters
you killed.

We have crafted thousands
of words together, you have
made me a thousand promises

Maybe they will come true,
tomorrow.

Type 510B

girl crawls into cat-skin
out of the cold.

girl is skinned
after her pussy is taken.

girl is taken
because they see only a lying suit (slut),

a girl who would seduce her father
for a kingdom, because they rationalise
running away as playing
hard to get.

girl must be clever
be after cock, money, power

girl must be lying,
ignore her, ignore the outfit that doesn't fit
the narrative.

girl lies with her body,
girl lies.

girl lies dead,

forgotten, replaceable
as a stray cat.

Base Twelve

Look at your hands,
count the bones with your thumbs.

Give it to me
your hand.

They used to have music for this
they had a dance for each phrase,
a whole language of bodies
of steps

    filled with things not meant to be said.

    They did not tell you?
    Do not speak of the branches
    brass, silver, gold.

They know how to gobble up sunlight
gobbler, like of food,
a feast, each night.

    Gobbler, like that you sip from Princess.
    You pay with your hours
    With your shoes.

    Feet are not hands.
    Careful not to wear them out,
    lest you have to run all the way
    home.

What is Grown

He tossed flowers
into our navels as we lay
under the dimming winter sun.

Covered us
with dirt and left us
to grow, to feed.

We whispered songs to our friends
the worms, and they joined us
in the chorus as we prayed

not for his life to bud,
and burst forth

but for the sun
to shine again—

perhaps on us.

Draconic

I am not a dragon
and so,

I am not breathing fire—
I am choking on it,

on the moments that pass too quickly
to be raged at

on the stumbling indecision of my own
tongue, unprepared to strike, unable to command
the fire that is my duty to my sisterhood
and so,

I am unable to go back, to find action
in time, to punish the wicked knights

who stick their swords into the bellies of women,
not beasts.

Shock

It is Winter— one season of four
in repetition, and I am shocked
a hundred times a day.

Electrons dance on my skin,
the cold air lacking
the density necessary to keep them
static as I reach:

for the brushed-steel kettle,
the door,
the comforting fur of a cat

A spark
—flinch—
repeat, repeat, repeat.

I sit down at my computer,
tremble at the first touch of fingertips
to keys after the sliding of my boots on carpet.

I open my browser,
electricity whirring behind the screen,
pixels forming into a headline:

"Expose!" a man,
artist, wielding
paintbrush, pen, pike

penis.

I read,
& I am not shocked.

Ophelia Complexes

perhaps all Great Artists have
at one point loved her sorrow.

there is something about drowned girls.

about women who fall
for the madness of men,

who suffer it —
flowers and all.

Traces

The seduction was another life ago
and yet you are still here
living men, on horses
finding your dreams before the women you rode to get there.

You are inconsequentially memorialised.
I am notches, images, evenings,
ephemeral.

I am songs,
I am less than I think I am.

I am not hashtags or links,
not laws, not honour,
not the future.

I am the barest sliver of the past —
not even her shuttle,
her loom, her scissors.

My place has never been in your bed,
on your cock, matron to your summer,
your time, your ghosts

and yet I find your carvings still upon the wood,
your hands still upon my body,
your words still lodged in my gums,
my cunt.

Sometimes I hear your song by accident
and I find my memory humming along,
for I do not get to ride away,
I only get to ride.

Beauty, Sleeping

Your mother-in-law eats you,
chews you out for breakfast
as though it was you who stole her son
and his virtue, though you were unconscious at the time.

This is a story she has folded into her bones,
and she is not the first to play
at owning her child's sex.

At dinner she puts you in the pot,
all meat, forgetting you are a vegetarian.

Still, you try:

You make her grandchildren,
let them and him both suckle you,
keep them all from screaming.

You trim the hedges to her specifications,
and do not let the years, or shelves gather
dust.

You keep his improprieties as concealed
as your wrinkles.

But she still asks
after your weariness,
suggests you get more sleep.

An Interrogation of Colour

My mother gives me a pie every year
for my birthday, in a Tupperware container,
in a basket, and she makes sure my clothes are not
red.

She leaves her name inscribed on the lid,
as though I could forget who it belongs to
even as her handiwork fills my belly, as I filled hers,
as my granny filled the wolf.

I step onto the bus, and it barrels down
its predetermined path, the same one it takes
every day. The wolf knows the schedule,
he too is a citizen of this city, has watched the forest
fall away to satellite maps and GPS schedules.

The doors close, and he sits beside me.
He does not wear his coat, but I know it is him—
from the loudness of his breath, the way he sets
his knee, too close, as though by accident.

I hold my goods closer, press up against the window,
hold my hand over the name of my mother, afraid,
knowing that we all get eaten regardless, but hoping
perhaps my hand will protect her
from the indirect predation of strangers.

He looks over my shoulder, and I think
at least the name is not my own. My mother has meat
on her bones, she crafts dough with her hands,
softer than mine. I am thankful that he does not reach
to touch mine, to find their callouses. I hold my breath,
press the bones of my knees together, and wonder
what colour she dressed in.

The Thousand-Year-Old Sexbot

She came out of flowers,
always flowers
or clay.

She came out of chrome and sculpted plastic,
out of god-given warmth
and impotent wet dreams.

He opened the petals,
plucked them in rhyme,
molded her with his hands

all before putting in breath,
a voice-box,
responses.

She came.

And he was praying
to his own creation,

And she, bewildered
said,

"made me…
you,

made me."

Lies Told to Thumbelina

There is no fact that says a woman must endure
a toad, a mole, the winter
before a faery prince may be hers
in desert.

No matter how mothers may whine
that their sons are lesser monsters
and that this is enough,
for them to be owed someone
petal-soft, made of care,
and kisses.

No matter how they say
that all we who are such may do is pray
for spring, for flowers to bloom.

That we may only hope
their opening is enough
like love.

Woman

They say that to be
a woman, is to be
a womb—

endless bounty, soft
suffering.

Prometheus was a Woman

The bird comes a-stabbing
with the moon, not the dawn
beak burrowed in our abdomens,
the liver mere metaphor
for polite company.

The regularity of pain is no accident,
nor are the chains. The punishment,
for fire or creation
it makes no difference:

we challenged prideful gods
with our god-given bodies, needful
of warmth and love, community,
growth, and so

we writhe on schedule
in penance, unable to return
our transgressions, stolen
or otherwise

our sins too entwined
to be et out.

 Blood Moon

My bones are smooth as clay;
hips, aching with the flexibility
these hormones bring along
with all the romance of blood

not half so poetic as you
starveling, breathless, and trembling
in wait, the magic mirror spasming.

"fairest, fairest,"

redder than her mouth,
redder than her womb,
redder than
redder

but do not paint the roses with that,
let the brush take your lust instead,
plant restraint and water it with kisses
nourish it with sacred time

give assignation, penance
in the light of a new colour.

Red

My mother was thirty-seven when she miscarried.

When my potential brothers
left, when my eleven-year-old sister found her on the kitchen floor
in a pool of her own blood, hair splayed.

When the paramedics carried her away
in a box of blinking lights
and blaring beeps.

I am fourteen, waking up in a pool of my own.

It is a monthly ritual:
Where I beg clothes, dry and unstained from my grandmother.
Where I run the washing machine at three-fucking-thirty-AM.

I will live this story on repeat for years,
count the months in sacrificed underwear,
tampon wrappers, and ibuprofen.

My best friend is twenty-two, she thinks of babies in numbers.

She does the math on the potentiality,
on the blood and tears, the days and work
that would need to be spent first — to even arrive at someday.

She tries to reconcile it, like she reconciles her taxes
like she reconciles her mother's work, how she is a product
of injections and time that she cannot spend as she wishes.

The princess is sixteen, she pricks her finger on a spindle.

A single drop of blood falls,
spatters onto the cold wooden floor.
She sleeps for a hundred years, for now.

I do not blame her.

Call to Action in Translation

Find me a new story to paint,
wine-dark, where they comb metaphors
instead of beaches, where the poets are not the only ones
bursting with heartache

where men do not make pigs
of themselves, both gentle and beastly,
where all the heroes come home,
and their wives do not know fear,
where the maids, virtuous in necessity
find more than agency in their adjectives.

In which swirling whirlpool does disaster lie?
All of them—
       so sort out meaning
       seek out new speech.

       There are other shores to adventure.

Listen, they are calling
       you.

Part 2: A Saga of Struggle

ichor and wine

my fingers are ash-stained,
the raw tips of them burn with salt
and the dryness of grip this season
brings. flaky claws, not sweaty
paws. still, they crumble the world
in a bowl, skin stripped, the marks
of individuality burned away
by friction alone. A different sort
of burn, new prometheus is born
keeping of liver, heart, and head,
revel, a moment more, a flick
sharp metal rolling down a mountain
did you not think we too
could set it all
on fire.

Hysteria

This is not an apology,
it is a warning.

You do not get to be afraid
of blood, you do not get to have
your ignorance, you do not deserve
an easy revolution.

We are here,
writhing, we have always been
here, building you.

We have always been giving
of our lives, our bodies,
our hours—

You cannot take our rage.

Third

There is a wave.

A wave made of hands
of feet, of ribs, of breasts
of hair. God, there is so much hair.

Some of it is long, some not.
All of it belongs to you. You, Woman.
You, Women.

It is your cast-offs. Your cut-offs.
The parts that did not fit,
the names beyond the initials,
the pseudonyms, the husbands.

It is the body that could not be taken
in miscredit.

What is put into the ocean will always come back to shore
eventually

I look out at the waves and I see what my mother could have been
if there was this density of pollution in her birth
if the saline levels had bucked the status quo.

Her hands are of the undertow,
they hold me, and I drift, belly up.

This wave is not for drowning,
This wave will bear me home.

Stone Cold

She tells the boys that snakes live between her thighs.

that hers are bigger
than any they might brandish.
that hers will bite
should they come too close.

She tells the boys that her moon blood is their venom.

that it is like acid
and will make them burn
and writhe if they dare
to touch her.

They say her mother is a monster, for teaching her such things.

her mother says they may laugh now,
but the first look her father
took of her turned him to stone
and if they try, they will wish to be
so lucky.

Particularities

She put a grain of sand
under my eyelid,
not a pea
under my mattress

and still, I do not sleep.

Each morning comes,
the performed joy of waking
for his honour, the unemotional tears
second, unbidden, borne of irritation
or exhaustion, I know not
which.

I yawn at the day
at how carefully they scrub my skin
how precisely they watch my hand
with the knife at the dinner table.

I never pretended to be a princess,
I just was a discomforted woman
—and that was enough for them to avoid
the cost of a corset.

Now I dream of bedding you,
how you will lick my face clean
again, give me new eyes
like a new name.

Our kingdom will be a hundred mattresses high
all of them waiting to be stained salty,
too uncomfortable to look
upon, and you will know

the grating that can keep you
from sleep.

The Yearly Pomegranate Poem

I am a glutton for the underworld,
finding my bones before their time
letting them s e p a r a t e into soup
washing them clean with pomegranate
juices, drowning as they burst

now satiated, as it is
a womanly way to go.

Apologies from the Moon

I met Daphne in the woods today.

She was clutching her stomach,
holding tight the things that were left to her.
The gnarls of her bark gripped tenuously to the gap
of innocence that remained.

She stood strong,
roots tangled in a pedestal of mud,
her atop it all-exposed
like she would not have wanted.

But I had brought only an apology, and not a shovel
so I could not shore up the remnants of her maidenhead,
could not build muddy walls
to keep this place clean.

I give this repentance to the ants,
so perhaps they might carve it into you, Daphne,
with their hunger and their teeth.

So perhaps someday when the rest of the world comes
to chop you down they will read that I was wrong, and so
they will change your form again.

They will turn you into a chair, or a cabinet,
or a boat; Finally, you will be inviolate
and the forest will remember the rest.

Visions

I want them empty,
but they are full.

I want a lack of lines
space, to roam in curves.

I want a world that does not
incite these kinds of angry tears;
a world where we do not
make places for people
all mapped-out roadways
and jurisdictions and over used tropes
and zoning houses and business
alike.

I want a place where my kind
was not cut from a rib
was not laid over the image of Earth
to likewise be pillaged and raped.

I want a place where I am allowed to want
emptiness, where it is without
further meaning.

Subversive Songs

I cannot sing walking songs with my voice,
they do not come in my range.

The adventures do not come for us,
the road is not the thing which sweeps our feet.

You do, and you pick us up
like princesses, and bring us
back home.

We are bodies of
intrigue, not days of forest water
and wild berries.

We are not the feet to get there,
we are home.

I have never found a treasure map,
never met a wise old man. But
I have lacked a home, and found
solace in the road.

And I would sing walking songs for
my own comfort, to stand against
fear, in my own voice.

Branched Longing

I might as well sit here and eat apples
because I was born with a heart
encased in ribs, they said once were someone else's.
And so, if I am to be the aggressor
and not the victim— if I am to be the person worthy of blame

I will at least enjoy the taste.

I will enjoy it even though I was lonely before I was born
and am lonely when I sleep,
and I know the sheets would be warmer
than I want them in the morning,
and colder than I want them
in the evening, if a figure were to lay his sin down
beside mine.

I will enjoy it, even if their body would fit
like seeds in my esophagus, and their arms
would be like the branches holding me
even if I was not what they were reaching for

even if they were reaching for the apples,
for all the metaphors that were ever written
over their red skins all those thousands of years ago

even if in that knowledge, there was no space left
in your hands for their deliciousness, or any other
type of story.

I will enjoy it even though I have broken bones
that were not ribs and I did not feel it,
even though I have tasted sin that wasn't sex
and I did not regret it

even though I loved a man that wasn't a god's son,
wasn't a god's creation, and I do not think I'll ever love
any person that is.

I will enjoy it because I was born here:
where they tell stories of apples and folly like it is a lesson,
like you are supposed to learn shame,
and regret the loss of ignorance.

I will enjoy it and I will climb apple trees,
I will eat the fruit in the branches, and let it drip
down my chin, my cleavage, my ribs

and tell you:

I do not mind if you blame me when I fall down
because I have been that much closer
to the sky.

For women who are not made out of metaphors

*"If you grow up the type men want to love,
you can let them love you"*
- Sarah Kay

No matter what pair of arms
tries to warm me
I am stone.

For him, I melted into a sphinx.
He rubbed his fingertips raw on my
sandy sides.

I gave him the word "No".
I gave him riddles I did not even know the answer to
because the only desire I could fulfill was the gift of a quest.
I will be gone when he returns for his prize.

For some I am a pillar,
they run their hands over my Ionic curves.
I do not move or speak.

They search for depth where there is none
they walk themselves around me while I am
rigid, holding up buildings against
the pressure of the sky.

For you I am a statue.
You grab me whole and drag me
to your Pygmalion's workshop.

My marble clothes billow against a wind
that does not exist
and for a moment when you touch me
I breathe, and shudder.

But I am a mountain
still made of stone.
I have myths in my valleys and
mysteries on my peaks.

I am too vast for any two hands
to hold.

Gluttony, and other Sins

I am Eve
in the Garden

chipmunk-cheeked,
juice spilling over the threshold
of my lips.

I am choking on the seeds
in my race to consume,

ravenously swallowing down
even the bark
wantonly torn from the tree.

I am belly-distended
from too much cyanide

but not from too much knowledge,
never, from too much knowledge.

A lack of excess

My ribs have been scooped out,
and there is song in the place
where marrow should be.

It sings that this empty buzz is no longer ice,
but water, that I have melted
into a lake.

That I can crown kings, or
drown sailors.

It tells me that my body is my own
and it is wide and deep; that there is nothing
to be carved away anymore

that there never was.

Searching for a new Lamppost

Susan returns,
to the smell of pine
and dreams that have crumbled
into sand, that have been judged
by time and found wanting.

She has committed the crime
of having taken too many steps,
too many kisses like plucked sour cloves,
once tucked into her childish cheeks,

until her mouth learned other uses
and someone said the rest had to be
forgotten,

until someone said that there were no more entrances
only exits, that the arrow had been flung
from a bow, her hands were now too big
to wield, and no one would make her
another.

Susan hikes the mountains,
strokes the moss along the stony banks
of the riverbed, searching for cracks,
for an opening to rest, for that perfect
patch of sunlight on the water
refracting up onto a corner of lichen-kissed stone
for a place that she could stay,

a place she could build
another life, like another world,
a summer that will not end
a home that is as strong as her heart.

She makes her own bow this time,
a birch bough door to independence,
the string woven hemp, simpler

than a unicorn's hair, but hers
from her hands, that she trusts,
that she knows will not shut
the way to any that follow,
her hands that open

and continue opening.

Lovers

You are a person
who had a childhood, who had a child's hands
that touched dirt and trees and other tiny, sticky hands.

You had your first kiss with your mouth.
You remember it
it is a part of you, a part of how you love.

Your favourite food is chocolate chip pancakes
because that is the taste your tongue likes best—
your tongue, that lives in your mouth
and tells you one-fifth of everything you know
—what you know, not what others have told you.

You do not own your body.
Your body owns you, owns everything you are
knows what it felt, what it taught you with its senses.

you have written yourself across your shins,
your fingerbones,
your pre-arthritic feet

you choose where they walk, what they touch
—so maybe "own" is wrong

it is your own, and you of it
you belong to each other

do not sell your lover short.

Partialities

It is like the buzz of True North

like the ease of conversation
from lips that have drunk
of time

like I am metal,
and flesh,
and woman

and know how to find home.

Part 3: The Lore of Love

Cinderella Sewed the First Dress

I would take the pumpkins
and the tears, like woven mist
and make of them my own ballgown

silky satin, made to be caught
on breezes, and twirl like summer.

The ball is never about the dance
it is about how it feels to be dancing:
you, falling in love with your own bones
the joy of it

that makes him fall in love with you
and all that you have built.

Odyssea

I want you bound
to me

mast tied, ears stuffed;
the same type of singularly
selfish goal, allowed
to experience your wonder
without any fear of being capsized
and left to founder in the water
of the knowledge
of the love

that I will drown in
without the security
of a Ulysses
pact.

Self-Made Slumber

I have pricked myself on your needle
one last time, and now you are off
to slay your dragons, leaving me
to my own —the dreaming kind—
no less terrifying or taloned.

If only it was only
sleep until once again I am
back in your arms, your touch watering
me back to life.

But alas, you are gone, along
with your thorn, and the sword
in my throat has no wielder
save sorrow, and a hundred years of dreaming logic
may be any time at all.

Maybe I surround myself
with the memory of you.

Build myself
a fence of brambles, water them
with my tears, each drop a story
of you, so they will know you
when you return,

so they will part
at your lightest touch
as I once did.

Howl

The Wind wants,
like the heart,
like worms, gluttons
on the rain until it makes bait of them.

It wants,
like *hunger*,
like a throat choking
on lover's words

until a girl, eyes wide
and too full, like the moon
howls in the night

lacking you, and so
is satiated only by screaming,
made drunk by naught but air,

as empty as all the rest of it.

Oysters

I am the otter at the bar,
outsourcing my cleverness with rocks
to the waitress,

sucking back the sea
that tastes like my mother.

She too, had two
skins, two
worlds, like two
genders.

One might think it double
the choice, double
the chance, double
the love.

But when has opportunity ever
overruled the harshness of fear,
the desire to control?

They locked her other-skin
in a box, put it somewhere
she never found,
lived a half-life
already buried.

I slurp another oyster.

They slip down like sorrow,
salty sustenance in the remembering,
in the hope that tomorrow
I will have choices that she did not

that I will crack my meat-skin open
and no one will care what is inside,
that it will taste like home

like not having to choose
the water or the land,
the azure blue or sunset pink

that a lover might not ask
which I am
before they swallow me.

Germ Lines

I am not seven generations
of seventh sons.

I am four generations
of eldest daughters.

Four generations of heirs
without namesakes
or curses, without gifts.

I am contrast, comparisons,
a different kind of lucky numeral

my lineage, interrupted.

Natural Killers

The ground of my family is death,
our inheritance a plague
of sterility,

the love we bear for our partners
reproducing until it becomes cancerous
growth

and must be ended.

My mother loved my father
like an ant loves its ophiocordyceps,
both infected by different kinds of poison;

he lost his spawn,
she, her mind.

My sister has a womb
always outgrowing itself.

It loves her, wants to make her body
of it. It latches
onto her intestines, her stomach

her body food
for the possibility of progeny,

each menstrual cycle a heaving squeeze,
which grows rampant, strangling itself.

In another life my uncle shattered
my aunt's hips with the weight of his
child, with the bearing
of all he wanted to make

and like when the earth gives way,
cracks in quakes, and nothing more
can grow until the dust settles.

The fragments of what used to be finds new homes
in the fissures, her first babies left to suckle
on the jagged edges.

Another uncle has been run dry,
a different aunt has cursed him
like he is some kind of village,
and the river that used to give it water
dried up, and will never again slake
the thirst of a desperate town.

It has irrigated all the life it ever will.

And we endure, bearing plague
upon our partners in our middle years—

gifting endings to our children,
cruel enough to see this suffering handed on

and down,
to bloom like bacteria, like viruses
like a witch's doom,

and there is nothing
more natural.

Stymphalian Mothers

someday they will wear through me.
their papery beaks carving all the way to
the other side of this diamond body
each peck a year, a page,
softly flipping.

did it start with my ear drum?
my navel? or was it
the sloping indent of my neck?

yes, it could be that my head will come clean off.
it may not be what I have
feared. it may not be the mottled, meaty horror that I cannot bear
to even look to check on.

sometimes they bring me gifts of worms.
Oh! Stymphalian mothers give me anything,
so long as you send me your children;
my elbows have grown used to your migration

each year. tell your spawn of my mountain,
let your flight paths be your legacy.
let me be the stone they sharpen themselves against.
without you I could not reckon the seconds of eternity

and so my ears have grown wanting
for the sound of your wings on the horizon.
the remnants of my intestines long
for the grip of your claws.

do not speak of extinction,
I would miss you.

Etumon

Then:

The sea roils,
wet, without care to electrocution
in irreverential abiogenesis.

Now:

He smooths the edges with His saw,
packs up dirt against the wound He has created

He marvels, reveling in the shadow of the new prosthesis
He has provided for the Earth.

She seeds His womb with electricity, running the wires
through this bodily extension.

She marvels, reveling in the light of invisible motion
She has gifted to His creation.

They kiss, as though they make
with love.

Tomorrow:

The organisms that remain call it giant.

Finally, it knows connection
through its extinguished light
and unlubricated limbs

the roots have sewn up the gash,
dusted with rusty sparkles

they weave it into the whole,
the shoreline continues gently

creeping ever upwards.

Meteoric

We are all born of certain seasons:
glass, iron, Fall, Spring.

Some babies are made of New Years,
or honeymoons, some of firsts,
or anniversaries.

Some are born under Jupiter,
some Mars—

there are so few planets for women,
only Venus
as if all our orbits were loving.

But I am writing ahead of myself.
There is no conception, there will never be.
There are only concepts.

My child,
you were born under a meteor
in a season of falling, wishing things.

I do not know what this means for your life,
but know, that you burn in my sky.

Weaves

You wear your sadness like a
cloak. careful crafted,
clever pockets
all stitched together, patchwork-

your mother would cry
at your handiwork.

Designed

A snip, so base.
An insertion.
A wail that does not yet exist.

She will only take her mother
— of her father, she will not
take the infection.

She will only take the life,
she will make it hers, someday.

For now she is only her substance,
defined in strings of letters,

but she has already worked the first magic
the first action of her cells
she has said "No."

Repetitions

The ballgowns come around each year,
the prince comes once a lifetime.

The slippery feelings,
the hauntings in the hills—
they never go away.

Sometimes, it is evening
and your bones are made of rocking chairs
and you forget what was said
because you didn't believe it the first time around.

Sometimes, the mother dies too often for it to be convenience,
and you make a new ending
because you do not want your daughter
to look at you with scissors in her eyes.

The convention is not convention,
it is yawning mothers who have not slept in a hundred years
too tired of making to come up with a new story this time.

Scented Wisdom

Potpourri is:

    the bailiwick of grandmothers
    of bowls living on tables close to death
    of halls meant for stays and sleep
    but never rest.

Never rest,
my child, for death sometimes smells sweet,
    sometimes is red, like lover's lips
    parted under sheets, still warm.
    Still to be opened like a flower in the morning.

Dry out your lovers,
so they will not rot.

Set them in crystal upon a table,
breath in, live beyond the cut stem,
in the pressed and sun-crinkled smell that remains.

Cut

sometimes,
in the dark I feel
a wizened crone

next to your sweet
summer child

I hold up my shears of knowledge,
of introspection to the blackness

unafraid of severing frayed ends.
I am Atropos, I am Urd.

I am the knower of all endings,
tender of the tree, woman beyond womb,
namer and shaper both.

Inheritances

I am carving a hole in your heart,
my darling

for it is the dearest gift I know
how to give

though I have lived its curse
know, that the shape of my handiwork
will ache forever.

Like I know that the blocks I make from the light
are of me, I can watch them collapse, fade to shadow
grow once more.

And I know, that adventures are lonely sorts of creatures.
That they are traumas,
that they end.

That eventually you and I must plod on
as though nothing has happened
even when the birds come and eat us away
tempted by the lacks we bleed from.

That we must not turn away from our lives,
from our selves. We must live in the ache
on the road that is not smooth,

bless our children with our shadows
and our knives.

Borne Fruits

I was born in the beginning of the dark.

Maybe, I would see the end
of this hundred year night.
Maybe, I said—
shoving away mortality as only mortals can.

We were told to live in the spaces
that eradicating wealth left, in
the rivets and screws that held
this metal box together

the way my hands held you.
Making a life of bodies, without
making myths of purposefulness,
eating the last of the pomegranate seeds

all twelve of them. And then I kissed you,
making no legacy. My mother never found me,
and I never saw the winter's end.

Part 4: Victorious Fictions

 Last Battles

I wonder if this is how magic fades:

with children dying before their parents,
with the slow extinction of tolerance and diversity.

with the taste of metal in water,
and disinterred graves
—bones, uprooted along with the flowers that graced them.

Patriotic

Countries are not born like people.

There is too much blood,
too many screams.
You have to decide
who you let in the room
and hope the nurses will listen.
But no one asks if the proclamations you make are fair.

After all, you are the one
giving birth— forget the fertile womb
of your own mother, that you were nourished
by someone, by the benevolence
of the land, that connections and infrastructure
brought it to your mouth
and let you grow into something
that could reproduce.

So what,
if all life begins
violently, and you were shot
from your mother like gunfire,
tore her apart like civil war, forget
that she kept you from plague with her antibodies,
as though genealogy
were pure, and linear.

And so you live,
while her body decays.

While it rots, you grow
inside of it, pressing the ribs open,
cracking her like an egg,
emerging to see she is only the latest

in a pile of bodies,
in a pile of lives

claimed, by someone else.

Historical

The stories we heard were only half-told.

And now, we are left
to reconstruct old wars
from their aftershocks.

To piece together histories
that were never written down,
that make myths of the present.

We work, with the tools of our archaeology
—we learn to not dismiss the dust
because we never made it a pharmaceutical,
because we don't have the language to differentiate
the soil from the silt.

We try to make old battlefields bloom,
we water them with the blood of our guilt.

We make new stories,
about the aftershocks of war,
fight over their meanings.

We fail, to ask the conquered for theirs,
the ones that were never written down.

August, The Apocalypse

The ground absorbs our sins,
gives back dizzy fumes
from hot asphalt, the seasons stuck

and waiting,

punishment for making ridicule
of growth, and blasphemy
of betterment

leaving only

bitter berries on the vine,
static in the wires,
and so many lives

unloved.

Canary Perfumes

I wonder if war is something you can smell.

If all the citizens in all the worlds have always
been able to sniff it out, know its approach
like garbage on a summer morning;
Sniff it, like they sniffed out dissent
and difference.

I wonder what it smells like.

I know it is not yet the tang of gunpowder and gas,
I know it is not yet the smell of dishonourable men and
rotting babies.

No, I imagine it more like the wafting of un-showered bodies
on the sidewalk, of moon blood
on women's clothes, of hot ink
on shredded newspapers, of ketones
in the urine of the hungry, but not yet starving.

Or perhaps it is like smog, like pollution
only palpable on the bad days, the days
that acid stings your eyeballs, the days
the posters go up.

 Security Theatre

We pull away,
but not from each other
    unstuck, from gravity,
if not the geography
of nationalism

so enmeshed as we are
in the industry of fear.

Do my breasts hold bombs?
Do my braids plot treason from their tower?
I do not know how touch assuages
these worries, grounded

we may never get there—
if we try, your sensibilities might pop

along with your ear drums, more delicate
still, and yet we might find equilibrium
    in flight, if only we tugged
free, with a little more violence.

Logic of a Suicide Bomber

We know existence
is no intrinsic good.

What is left?
When they take
      your body,
      your freedom,
      your family,

when you have the opportunity
to have your life ring out
a message:
      "not this."

If you will not listen to my pleas
then hear my silence,
my lack of screams

plead your own ignorance
(as I know you will)
when you ask the fire,
the shrapnel

why I wanted this.

Resignation Syndrome

What of an apple:
    Her lips, always red, always open;
    Her eyes, always closed
    away from the horror that has brought her here
    to the land of snow angels,
    away from the stepmother of civil war
    to where they made the bombs.

What of a boy named Georgi:
    His throat, pale and choked.
    You sent the huntsman after him
    to check his papers.

How would you hold this rejection?
How would you roll it through your teeth,
sluice it through them, let it caress
the yellowed pearls that are left?

He knows that soon it will taste like war again,
like gunpowder, like poisons that he cannot name,
because there were no schools to teach him Chemistry
except that classroom of sky,
where the lessons are led by his burning lungs,
and the peeling boils of his gasping skin.

I suppose to you it only tastes like apple seeds.
Limp bodies are so much harder to carry than guilt.

And so you blame them. You say,
"Why did you not have the decency to get to rigor mortis?
Why are you not far away where I do not have to look at you?
You ugly girl, you ugly death."
And here I thought you were good at looking in mirrors.

But I must be wrong, because you are still gazing at yourself
as you say,
"Send back the children!
Do not pop the seeds from their esophagi.
Do not show mercy."

Later, you comment to your glass reflection,
You say
"Doesn't the paleness of death
make them prettier?
They fit better when they are white."

You bemoan a lack of space,
ignore the connection between the laces you threaded
and the shallowness of their breathing.
Now, you try to feed them apples
forgetting what their redness, their malus has always meant

You hope no princes see their bodies
hope the dwarves do not make their coffins out of glass
hope the Kings do not see your ugliness,
hope that they too are wicked.

Human Devastation Syndrome

The nightmare was long,
the sleep,
long.

Three years of violence
may well have been a hundred.

The others have had children
to suckle them back to this world,
themselves, the byproducts of violences
done upon women's bodies.

She has only an uncle.

"Speak, Souhayla,"
              he says.

But she has not used her throat in a hundred years.

There are generations of violence
and generations of redemption.

You are here,
you are safe now,
you are awake.

You had no fairy blessing,
no thorns to cover you with the safety of spikes,
only sleep.

We do not invent new tales,
new heroes. Only new words,
words like, "Human Devastation Syndrome."
words like, "Severe Shock."

They are not enough.

Burning all the spindles in the world
would not be enough,

and perhaps we all look like ogres
from the other side of that nightmare-
beasts with fleshy hungers to fill.

About the Mirror's Pieces

You sent the four winds blowing
to find safe harbor, for you,
for your child.

They came back, whispering of mountains,
and blew, and blew, and blew you along
into the hands of unkindly robbers

no shards of glass needed for your eyes
to find their disillusionment,
no hardness to be plunged in your heart
except that of suffering, to insulate against the kiss
of cold.

The peaks are conduits, with demons at their zenith
unable to fully ascend to a mockery of God.

My tears cannot wash this sorrow from your eyes,
frozen as they are in the night, too tired
as you were to complete the mosaic of escape
the rules of the Snow Queen as lying as nature.

The road is never easy, but the wind cannot know that,
looking as it does to a girl with a frost-burned face
seeing only strength, only survival, only tears
for the snatched ones she was not made to rescue:

A family of snowflakes,
and dreams of the other side.

Roxham Road

In upstate New York there is a road
that ends.

Hundreds walk upon it
following past the hard line of cement
following the small white pebbles the children left
to light the way.

Their mother died before the story began
and their father could not withstand the hurricane.
Their stepmother? Well, you have heard of her.

She tells you she is freedom
but she is bullets and discrimination,
she is careless, wicked.

And the children from other wombs,
other lands? They do not deserve her space,
her time, her pity. She does not have to look upon them.

So they walk on, past where the road ends.
They go on to the prison of gingerbread houses,
give their hands up to be arrested.

They hope that witches are kinder,
that the food she feeds them is without further purposes,
that she is satisfied with the imprisonment of candy canes
and the fragility of their sugar-spun sentiments
is better sustenance than deportation.

Sécurité

The first thing they do is hang you
by your shoulders

you did not know it would be like bracelets
too high up, on the inside. that you would feel
yourself a suit of armour, segmented
at each joint.

They do this so you lose your sense
of touch, this opening

of your chest, to bare it
worldly, to bring in to embrace
all the way down to your fingers, phalanges,
giving you language for reaching, out.

Next comes the muzzle,
they do not let you keep

the dignity of your screams, evidence
in the constancy of your protest, resistance
in the chorus of hoarse dedications that would flow forth,
spitting truths.

The dead possibility of your speech lies beside you,
foreshadowing.

Would that you were only a witch,
burning would be faster, or a warrior,
because at least then this would be for your comrades
and they could topple empires with their love affairs,
bring the babies home in your stead.

Your mother rocked you once.
She would take you by your arms and swing you,
you, bright-eyed, would giggle
joyful in the lack beneath your feet
the air between your body and limbs perfectly outlined,
ambient with the universe.

I promise you will return there, even
if you have to climb. One day they will step back
and see the mountain you beat through,
a thousand billion years of clipped beaks
and bloody sockets where your torso should have reach.

This age is golden,
just like all the rest of them.

They have taken you, shining,
unarmed, magical
only in the beauty of your existence.

Hush, think of these things, and not what happens next.
Here, a kiss,

before it starts.

Altweibersommer

Half-dead things rot in the sun
there is no wind to blow their crispness far from the cities
nor frost to ice them in preparation for their burial.

The children only scream until sunset—
it comes earlier than the dawn.

There are few leaves to shelter the end of the harvest
so pluck your gourds early before they turn to mush in your fields
and import your hurricanes,

ignore scarcity if it is in other places,
sweep what is left into paper bags
and leave them at the curb

hope in the meantime they do not burn.

Part 5: A Refuge of Tales

Look Homewards

Look homewards
and you will see a dragon;
widdershins, a mirror.

We are all just trying to keep our substance
through the winter.

We hum a tune, refining
pitch, trying to fit notes
into the underlying frame that supports
the metal joints this city walks on.

Do not look for eggs,
its biologic clock ticked dry before I was born.

This is not the time to consider
new generations. This is when
cement props up old veins pasted over with weight sensors

until they overflow, rubber on sidewalks,
glass in children's mouths and still it does not burn.

The dragon sits there, and picks its teeth
with a lying signpost— arrival times and all.
It belches, and I do not notice the smell.

The Earth sleeps, digests,
without attention to the direction of its rotation

it has already made its children, let them go
hungry without dinner, and fat can only insulate you
from so much.

Please

She is Cassandra-level prescient
walking the streets at midnight,
raving, right.

Naming the blue deaths,
and the cold ones

(you might not think that prediction hard,
but she's the only one who does it)
and she is always too late.

She comes to the Town Hall,
carries a petition with ten billion signatures
from all the people not yet born.

"Please,"
    she says.

"Do you love
    your fountain,
    your city,
    your legacy?"

and shows them what it looks like
if nothing changes.

The reply comes,

"Apply for a historical site designation.
Next!"

but she knows that next only goes
so far

that someday
ends.

Supplicant

The beggars here prostrate themselves
as though praying to a god
any passerby could become

each one of them
could bless them
raise them up

charity and divinity
a symbiotic loop
created with a simple coin
in the face of evil,
of suffering

but we have said that God is dead
and charity is foolishness,
and so there are only the demons

who walk past, cackling, hedonistic
torturing the worshipers
with the aversion of our gaze
our pity, that does everything
but give.

Spare Change

They take the dregs of our luxuries,
return them, process
to spare change.

Their wealth,
like our sparkling sticks, flashing,
then burning down, like the girl

—a dream, from childhood
dying for lack of any other warmth.

These things stay with you.
They are not like matches,
like matches are not flames.

A flame needs fuel,
like good sex needs passion.

Ah yes, we are back to a story you know,
wrapped in the comfort of champagne

looking off the edge of an old year,
looking to your lover
the flare of their lips as you say
"the future will be better."

You step out into the cold,
refuse it with intoxication,
which is more forgivable than the reason
you refuse the log shaped human

sleeping on the sidewalk
and you curse him, not even as gently
as you cussed out the troll under the bridge
on the way to the party.

Remember your fantasy at the beginning
of the night?

The dress you donned without a fairy godmother,
and here you are, home from the ball
past midnight

you helped no beggar, had no gems
placed on your tongue in thanks, or snakes
in retribution

you go home and have a happy ending anyways,
wake up to a new year, a new world
where only the wind sounds like screaming—

the rest of the voices frozen
in the night.

Gore Park

The fountain turned off today,
the last browning petals told us
so, even if the sun and its angel
clouds did not.

The city left the pillars,
the small air currents
for the polished metal and half-dried
cement, the lights left empty.

The circle of benches still
stands, its citizens still
staring at the congregations
that could have been.

Stand here and tell me you do not see it
:the lottery, the spectacle, the punishment
in the empty bowl,
thrice perimetered.

Sit here, stay;
the bench is long enough to sleep
on, the bowl is alcove enough to shelter
in.

Keep time, leave;
before the fountain turns back on.

Hamilton Harbour

The fires at the edge
of the water tempt
drowning men
to stay.

The harbour has sunk
a thousand dreams

steel bent
into art
into inequity

The pathways crumble
giving way to communities
of animalistic fey

reminding us
that even in our urban jungle
the lake is wild, and can flood
our hopes, our indulgences

leaving us all beggars
on half-submerged benches.

Countries of Geese

The honks cry out
just not for sweaters,
those would not end the course

they cry for a country
where they might not be called vermin
where protecting their goslings
would not be taken as violence

a country where everyone might have
a green patch, a flower
to eat, clean water
to swim in, and sky above

to fly away into
when it is time.

The Flamborough Dinosaurs

In my youth
we passed the land of dinosaurs
on our way to the white
snow hills

to bathe in the wind
of our frailty, to learn
bent-kneed fear, and practice
the slaloming lines of courage.

Now adult,
I tread the path again
see the paint that has flaked
the brontosaurus resting on his side

his head and chest to the ground
his long neck a bridge between them sloping
downward.

I know he will not rise
with gangly legs to continue
to grow old.

He has only the white of oblivion,
and I am practiced at courage,
but somehow,

this sunny disrepair is sadder
than all the bones.

Things that can only be once

the sky is cotton candy
if you do not look beyond the tree line
—over there it is burning.

over there, just through the gaps
in the foliage. above, there are wings
and tails, covered in sweet thick air
flying in asymmetrical arrows

running off to some other burning place

over there, beyond the houses
no gaps between them, to see
through, except if you jumped
one attic window to the next

raccoons, rat traps, chicken bones and all.

you could search there,
find a ring that was your grandmother's
give it to a girl you love, find
so many puddles with her

find a place you could eat the sky

where fire does not burn
—but the clouds would not taste
the same, and bodies like the waft

of heat.

Vast, Uncountable Things

The field of stars never ends.

They said it was out there:
a new world, and we passed
the point of no return
generations before

I was born.
But our planet blew up,
both of them—
the Old Country, and the New,

and now we are nothing but language
echoing across space,
never to land.

We imagine we are crossing
the sea, like our forebears,
that each twinkling star is a fish
swimming in the universe.

Our children play make believe
about fishes. We play make believe
about an end.

 Prayer

We all sing—
full-throated, high, raspy,
old whispers,

then we drop our blood
into the bucket
like it's pain.

The ritual is a transmission,
a prayer, that the aliens
aren't aware of xenophobia.

It is a hope,
that they are tempted
by our offering,

what we can give:
the scent of suffering,
the sound of despair.

It is a hope,
that they have pity,
pity would be better

than this, than what we have done.

Do not let this come from guilt

The clouds make lies of the rain,
while not-small-enough girls long after sweaters.

the world does not wish it was otherwise
—and neither do we, not really
we wish we had been otherwise

or that our parents had been,
that the story had not started in such an ugly place,
that the moon hanging in the afternoon sky did not
make everything else gray

the world does not apologise
so we must.

Smaller Eternities

I found a buried box.
In it, there were candies.

Candies, that tasted like flowers,
sweet, like they used to smell.

You were telling me about
the end of empires, talking

about living underground, unable to wait
for a call, but being able to feel
the Earth, rumble in your bones;

knowing that there were dragons outside,
knowing, that our miracle was tasting flowers.

Care

I want to speckle stars
on your lungs

to remind them:
there is no gravity in space.

Someday, we will get there.
and aeons after, when I am gone
they will remind you what I have said.

"You were made for sieges,
my darling,

You will outlast this war."

You will outlast
This war.

a clock ticks

a clock ticks
a man dies
a child, swollen bellied, hungers.

the chatter remains,
coming not with ease,
but routine.

the coffee shop is closed this week
and yet we still find ways to twitch-
fill our goals with excuses
our knuckles with turmoil

lick, thumb, flip.

give your words to the birds
instead of your boss.

they will listen, give you hope
and stitch it into your mother's dress

leave the lights up past the season,
call them fey,
call them

listen as the clock winds down,
the chatter dies,
do not be afraid
to answer.

Acknowledgements

First of all, I'd like to thank Nathan Caro Frechette of Renaissance Press, and the Ontario Arts Council for their recommender grant program, both of whom without which this volume would not exist. I'd also like to thank Joel Balkovec and Marjolaine Lafrenière, for their invaluable work in the editing of this manuscript, my dear friend Robyn Lightwalker for her stunning cover, and Ashley Hisson for turning me onto the recommender program in the first place. This work would not be possible without the work of so many writers before me, unnamed ones, and lost ones, those who have previously played with tropes and tangled with the myths that inform this work. Similarly, it would not exist without the support of my incredible partner, Michael Birch, and the work of many mentors over the years including, Christi Nogle and the SFWA mentor program, Mrs. Hubbard and Mr. Soderholm of the Beamsville District Secondary School, The Hamilton Poetry Society, Moon Milk, and the very kind man whose name I cannot recall who ran the Teen Poetry Club at the St. Catharine's Public Library when I was just discovering myself as a poet from 2007-2010. Likewise, there are innumerable folxs who have encouraged my work through kind feedback, reviews, and commentary, including Selena Middleton, Robert J. Sawyer, Joe Stacy, and numerous editors at magazines I have been fortunate enough to publish with, and for their encouragement I am endlessly grateful. Finally, there is my family: my mother, Nathalie Brown, grandparents, Susan and Clifton Brown, and best friend, Cassandra McLelland whose praise I will never believe but is nonetheless, like them, invaluable.

"Apologies from the Moon" first appeared in Wild Musette October 2017
"Particularities" first appeared in Dreams and Nightmares October 2018
"Draconic" first appeared in the University of Waterloo's *HeforShe Anthology* April 2019

"Beauty, Sleeping" first appeared in Augur July 2019

"Call to Action — In Translation" first appeared in Arsenika September 2019

"Stone Cold" first appeared in Truancy December 2019

"Vast, Uncountable Things" first appeared in New Myth's *Twilight Worlds*

"What is Grown" first appeared in Dreams and Nightmares May 2020

"Resignation Syndrome" first appeared in Truancy August 2020

About the Author

Lynne Sargent is a writer, aerialist, and philosophy Ph.D student currently studying at the University of Waterloo. Their works have appeared in venues such as Strange Horizons, Wild Musette, and Augur Magazine, and have been nominated for Aurora and Rhysling awards. *A Refuge of Tales* is their first poetry collection, and it was funded through an Ontario Arts Council Recommender Grant. To find out more, visit them on Twitter @SamLynneS, or for a complete bibliography visit scribbledshadows.wordpress.com.

Renaissance was founded in May 2013 by a group of friends who wanted to publish and market those stories which don't always fit neatly in a genre, or a niche, or a demographic. We weren't sure what we wanted to publish exactly, so like the happy panbibliophiles that we are, we opened our submissions, with no other personal guideline than finding a Canadian book we would fall in love with enough that we would want to publish and sell.

Five years later, this is still very true; however, we've also noticed an interesting trend in what we tended to publish. It turns out that we are naturally drawn to the voices of those who are members of a marginalized group (especially people with disabilities and LGBTQIAPP2+ people), and these are the voices we want to continue to uplift.

To us, Renaissance isn't just a business; it's a family. Being authors and artists ourselves, we are always careful to center the experience of the author above all else.

pressesrenaissancepress.ca
pressesrenaissancepress@gmail.com

If you enjoyed this book, please consider leaving a review where you bought it!

Whispers Between Fairies

Derek Newman-Stille and Nathan Caro Fréchette

Fairy tales have grown with us over history and changed over the years to capture the human experience. Yet, we often trap fairy tales in the past, calling them "tradition", and it means that certain tales don't get told. Nathan Frechette and Derek Newman-Stille bring out new tales from the old, telling stories from the voices that often aren't heard.

Whispers Between Fairies is a conversation between two authors who love fairy tales and each author takes their own path to find the hidden possibilities for each fairy tale. These are tales of beauty and enchantment... but they are also tales of darkness and secrecy, much like the original fairy tales. They are echoes of the past, but also firm reminders of the magnificent diversity of the present, exploring BIPOC, Queer, Trans, Disabled, and Mad experiences.

Sit back and let our words be a spell that brings you to worlds of enchantment.

pressesrenaissancepress.ca

NOTHING WITHOUT US

CAIT GORDON AND TALIA C. JOHNSON

We are the heroes, not the sidekicks.

"Can you recommend fiction that has main characters who are like us?" This is a question we who are disabled, Deaf, neurodiverse, Spoonie, and/or who manage mental illness ask way too often. Typically, we're faced with stories about us crafted by people who really don't get us. We're turned into pathetic, tragic souls; we merely exist to inspire the abled main characters to thrive; or even worse, we're to overcome "what's wrong with us" and be cured. Nothing Without Us combines both realistic and speculative fiction, starring protagonists who are written "by us and for us." From hospital halls to jungle villages, from within the fantastical plane to deep into outer space, our heroes take us on a journey, make us think, and prompt us to cheer them on. These are bold tales, told in our voices, which are important for everyone to experience.

pressesrenaissancepress.ca

www.ingramcontent.com/pod-product-compliance
Lightning Source LLC
LaVergne TN
LVHW052032080426
835513LV00018B/2292